# THE LORD
# HEARD
# MY CRY

# THE LORD HEARD MY CRY

Charles E. Green

PROVIDENCE HOUSE PUBLISHERS
Franklin, Tennessee

Published by
PROVIDENCE HOUSE PUBLISHERS
P.O. Box 158 • 238 Seaboard Lane
Franklin, Tennessee  37067
800-321-5692

# To My Sixteen Grandchildren and One Great-Grandchild

Susan Faye David
Jennifer Ann David Johnson
Michael Thomas David
Charles "Chuck" Robert Green
Laura Elizabeth Green
Andrew Porter Green
Laura Brook Johnson
Jennifer Lacey Johnson
Andrew Baylor Johnson
Ashley Barrett Johnson
Auburn Leigh Johnson
Allison Elaine Whaylen
Ryan Paul Whaylen
George Andrew Horton
Mary Beth Horton
Sarah Deedee Horton
Braelyn Ann Johnson, Great-Granddaughter

To share with my sixteen grandchildren and newborn great-granddaughter (September 17, 1995) that without a father or grandfather to help me, I asked God Almighty, my Heavenly Father, to help me, and through prayer, hard work, and study, I graduated with my M.D. in 1942.

*Charles E. Green and his grandson Ryan Paul Whaylen.*

# Contents

*Five of Charles E. Green's grandchildren at Halloween 1992, clockwise from top left: Laura, Jennifer, Auburn, Baylor, and Ashley Johnson. (Photograph by Madearis Photography Studio, Arlington, Texas. Used by permission.)*

# Foreword

IT HAS BEEN MY PRIVILEGE TO KNOW CHARLES
Green for about sixty years. Despite seemingly insurmount-
able odds, he went from the "cotton patch" to achieve a dual
ministry which, to my knowledge, is without parallel. We
became acquainted as students at the Southern Baptist
Theological Seminary in Louisville, Kentucky. Following his
graduation with a Master of Theology degree in 1937, he entered
the School of Medicine of the University of Indiana, where he
received his Doctor of Medicine degree in 1942. His goal was to
spend his life as a medical missionary in China.

After his graduation, Green was taken into medical military
service during World War II. He related to me his hope to be
sent to the Burma-China Theater where, at least, he could be
learning the Chinese language. Instead, he was assigned to a
submarine watch group stationed in the Puerto Rico-Caribbean
area. During the war, he saw only one submarine on the far
horizon. By the end of the war, communists had taken over
China, so that door was closed. Theron Rankin, secretary of the
Southern Baptist Foreign Mission Board, advised Green to set

up his medical practice in Oklahoma and be a missionary at home; this he did par excellence.

Recognitions which have come to Green speak more eloquently than my words. In 1963 Oklahoma Baptist University declared Green its outstanding alumnus and the greatest humanitarian in Southwest Oklahoma.

He served from 1969 to 1979 on the Board of Trustees of the Southern Baptist Hospital, New Orleans, and for two terms on the Board of Trustees of Oklahoma Baptist University, one term as its chairman. Without remuneration, he served for twenty-five years as camp physician for Falls Creek Baptist Assembly, summer encampment for the Baptist General Convention of Oklahoma.

In 1986 the High School Coaches' Association voted him into the Oklahoma Hall of Fame (the only physician to be admitted) for his service to school athletic programs. In 1989 the Oklahoma Medical Association awarded him the A. H. Robins Award as outstanding physician in Oklahoma for community service.

In 1994 the Mayor and United Way Trustees of Lawton honored Green as the outstanding citizen of Lawton for forty-five years of community service.

This book is the record of what God can do with one little boy in a cotton patch who is wholly dedicated to doing his will. Reading it will enrich your life beyond measure.

Herschel H. Hobbs<br>
Pastor Emeritus<br>
First Baptist Church<br>
Oklahoma City, Oklahoma

# Preface

A TRUE STORY OF A FOURTEEN-YEAR-OLD BOY who was abandoned by his father and cried out to Almighty God for help. God heard his cry, and his providential hand led him from a cotton patch in Southwest Oklahoma to Indiana University School of Medicine, where he received an M.D. degree in the class of 1942.

*Mary Beth Horton*

*Sarah Deedee Horton*

*Allison Whaylen*

*Three of Charles E. Green's granddaughters.*

# Acknowledgments

BERTHA PENDLETON GREEN BROOKS—My mother, who stayed by her five children, helped us survive the Great Depression, and gave us hope for the future.

JENNIE SULLIVAN GREEN—My wife of over fifty-four years and mother of our five children. She gave me love, hope, and encouragement to complete this book.

D. E. TROOP—My Sunday School teacher who won me to Christ and walked with me down the church aisle to give my heart and life to Christ Jesus.

T. B. HOLCOMB—My pastor who baptized me and gave me encouragement to enter the ministry.

W. A. WILCOXSON—Preached at my ordination and helped conduct my wedding to Jennie Sullivan.

E. E. HALLOCK—My pastor at Norman, Oklahoma, while I was a student at Oklahoma University. He gave me some of his sermons for me to use in my first revival in a country church near Norman.

GEORGE A. RITCHEY—He came to Oklahoma Baptist Univeristy my senior year and gave me a full scholarship to the Southern Baptist Theological Seminary in Louisville, Kentucky. He took me to the Paragon Baptist Church in Paragon, Indiana, and urged them to call me as pastor. They called me and helped make it possible for me to receive my Master of Theology degree at the seminary and my M.D. at Indiana University.

CLAYTON WADDELL AND INEZ LITTEN—Their marriage and friendship through the years have strengthened my spiritual life.

PAULA ROSS—Daughter of my sister Pauline, she, her husband Mike, and their children, Kelly, Ryan, and Nikki, have given me a home in which to relax in Florida, and she typed and recorded a long manuscript for this book.

CHERYL BROWN—She helped type my short manuscript.

LADONNA AND BEVERLY—Both did a tremendous amount of typing for this book.

HOOD WHICKER—He helped me put my book together.

JOHN PENNOI—He assisted in typing part of my manuscript in its early stages.

GARY AND LINDA COOK—My pastor and his wife.

CHAPTER 1

# Family Beginnings in Oklahoma

I WAS BORN IN ADA, OKLAHOMA, ON APRIL 20, 1911. My parents were Charles H. and Bertha Pendleton Green. The Pendleton family came from Fort Smith, Arkansas. My father came from Dalton, Georgia, where all the Green boys and girls were raised. I had an older sister called Ruby and two younger sisters, Pauline and Juanita. And the youngest of the family was my brother, James.

When I was a young child, we moved from Ada to Lawrence, Oklahoma, a small town south of Ada. My father worked there in the rock crusher. My older sister, Ruby, and I started school in Lawrence, and I finished the second grade in that locality. All I remember about World War I was that my mother and the other women sat up late at night knitting socks for the American boys in the trenches in France.

In 1919 my father moved the family to a "boom town" called Burkburnett, Texas. He was able to purchase a World War I quad tent—a tent with a center pole. The family lived in that tent most of the summer of 1919. Mother had to cook outside, and the four children slept on pallets. My mother and

15

father slept on iron cots. A center pole in a quad tent has a flap over the top to let the hot air out at night. One night we had a rain storm, and my father awakened me and pushed me up through the opening to pull the flap over the center pole to keep the rain from coming in. That was the first time I was baptized in a Texas gully-washer.

When September came, my father put the family on a train, and we went from Burkburnett to Lawton, Oklahoma. We found a house at the corner of 6th and E Street. We were enrolled in McKinley School, which was in the northeast corner of Lawton. I was in the third grade and was assigned a seat behind W. W. Greb. Bill Greb became one of my closest friends and has been my certified public accountant for over forty years.

McKinley School was known as a rather tough school. After school hours, Bill Greb and I would watch the older boys fight for their girlfriends. That was the big sport back in those days.

The next year we moved to 6th and H Street, south of the tracks, and in the fourth grade I attended Lincoln School. Most of the first semester my father took us east of Lawton to pick cotton. I returned to Lincoln in the second semester, but at the end of the school year, my teacher, Mrs. Bailey, said, "Charles, I don't think you should be promoted to the fifth grade, so I'm going to ask that you repeat the fourth grade." That was my first big disappointment. I told her the only person I hated to tell was my mother. But I did repeat the fourth grade at Lincoln, and I have never regretted that Mrs. Bailey made that decision.

I finished the sixth grade at Lincoln. In my class was Howard Angus, another young man destined to be a physician. Also in that class was one of my dearest friends, Maurice Meyer, who was the first person in Lawton to invite me to a Sunday School class in the First Baptist Church of Lawton. I attended Sunday School and was a member of Mrs. Asa Wilson's class. What I remember most was that she had a Franklin Steamer car, and she would take all of us boys fishing at Lake Lawtonka every Saturday.

I enrolled in Lawton Junior High in the fall of 1924 and completed the seventh grade. I entered eighth grade in the fall of 1925 and had gone to school about three weeks when my mother gave us children some bad news.

CHAPTER 2

# The Wake-up Call

WHEN MY MOTHER AWAKENED ALL FIVE OF US children early one morning in late September 1925, she told us that our father had gone to California to work in the oil fields; we had not heard from him in several months. The small amount of money that he left us was exhausted. Mother informed us that our only hope for survival was to hit the cotton patch.

That morning I went to Lawton Junior High, cleaned out my locker, and turned in my football equipment to my coach, Mr. Buckingham. My sisters, Pauline and Juanita, also terminated their schoolwork by telling their teachers that we would be leaving Lawton.

I thought, "Why is this happening to me?" It is an age-old question that many teenagers have asked, and it came home to me that I would be leaving school and giving up my friends because my father had abandoned us. The other boys in my class were enjoying wonderful, caring dads. I always envied Jack Love, for his father would be waiting on the sidelines after every football game, and at the end of the game he would give his boy a big bear hug whether we won or lost. Unfortunately, my father never saw me play a football game in junior high or high school.

My mother had corresponded with a cousin, Molly Thompson, who lived eight miles west of Apache. Mother told her that we needed jobs in the cotton fields, and she wrote back that a neighbor by the name of Arthur Lewis was looking for cotton pickers, and she felt sure we could fill the bill. On a Saturday morning her husband, Henry Thompson, came to Lawton to pick us up and take us to Apache. My mother and my two sisters rode in the back seat of the Model-T Ford with all our belongings: clothes, quilts, and blankets. James, my younger brother, who was four, and I rode in the front seat.

We arrived at the Thompson farm, and cousin Molly had a wonderful meal awaiting us. We were then taken to a farmhouse where we would live for the next six weeks as cotton pickers for Arthur Lewis. He and his wife were gracious people and gave us enough groceries to last until we could pick enough cotton to pay for our commodities.

Each morning we would rise early, Mother would have a good breakfast for us, and then we would go to the cotton patch with a sack lunch and work until sundown. The days were long and tough, and some of the mornings were rather cool. Our hands became numb and sore from the long days in the cotton patch.

Every Saturday night, Mother would fill a big galvanized washtub with water from the reservoir of the kitchen range, and we would all take our Saturday night baths. James and I would take our baths first. Then we would put on our winter underwear and head for our featherbed in the north bedroom.

While we were picking cotton, one morning a friend came by the cotton patch and asked me what I was going to be when I grew up. I informed him that I was not going to be a cotton picker. I was going to medical school and be a physician.

He told me that without a dad and having to work in a cotton patch, it would be a long journey to medical school. And that was where I first prayed and hoped. I cried out unto Almighty God for help. He inclined his ear to me and heard my cry. And the providential hand of a loving God would lead me from a

*Charles and Jennie Green standing in a cotton field owned by Elmer and Armilda Holsey—similar to the one in which he worked as a teenager in 1925 to help save his family from poverty.*

cotton patch in Southwest Oklahoma to Indiana University, where I would receive my M.D. in the class of May 1942.

By about the second week in November, we had saved enough money to return to Lawton, Oklahoma, our home. I started again in the eighth grade, and my two sisters resumed their school work. My older sister, Ruby, had remained in Lawton with friends and worked at the Tip Top Laundry. Several teachers were kind to me and helped me catch up with my school work.

When I was fifteen years old, my Sunday School teacher, D. E. Troop, said, "Charles, you're the only boy in our class that has never been baptized, and I want to see you follow the Lord Jesus all the way through the baptismal waters." I said, "Mr. Troop, I am a little scared. I don't have a dad to walk with me down that aisle and give my hand to Brother Holcomb and tell him I want to be baptized." That Sunday morning Troop put his arm around me and said, "Charles, I will walk with you." I was baptized on November 24, 1925, by Brother T. B. Holcomb.

CHAPTER 3

# Lawton High School Days

IN THE FALL OF 1926, I ENTERED THE NINTH GRADE at Lawton High School. At all the assembly programs, the ninth graders sat in the balcony, and we had a good view of all the activities. During my ninth-grade days, I decided that I wanted to play football, and I went out for practice with another classmate, Cash Gentry. I did not letter, but Cash made a great player and became one of the few athletes who ever lettered four years in football at Lawton High.

In 1927 I started my sophomore year at Lawton. Bryan Griffin was our football coach. I made all the trips as a second-team center, but only played in four games and did not letter as a varsity athlete.

My algebra teacher was Mary Louise Green from Waurika, Oklahoma. She was a beautiful lady and a wonderful teacher, and all of us boys had a crush on her. But every afternoon a young fellow would come to the east side of Lawton High School in a yellow roadster and pick her up. His name was E. E. Neptune; they later were married and had two outstanding boys. Bill Neptune became a chemistry teacher at

Oklahoma Baptist University. Dick became principal of Eisenhower High School and then superintendent of the Lawton Schools.

I have had the privilege of working with two young men during my lifetime who were selected as outstanding school superintendents of the nation: Dick Neptune and another young man, David Spencer, from Pontiac, Michigan. When I was pastor of a little Baptist church in Plainfield, Indiana, one of the pillar families of the church was the Luther Spencer family. They had three children, the youngest of whom was David. Before I left the pastorate, I had the privilege of baptizing him. He chose education as his calling.

Then when the awards for Outstanding Superintendents were given at a meeting in California, Dick Neptune saw a man across the table from him squinting at his identification sticker. As the two men engaged in conversation, David asked Dick, "Do you know Dr. Charles Green there in Lawton"? Dick replied that he certainly did, "He was my pediatrician!" I felt so humbled and honored to have had a small part in the lives of the two youngsters who had grown up to serve their communities so well they had this great honor bestowed upon them.

In the fall of 1928, I enrolled in Lawton High as a junior. Having decided to go into medicine, I took chemistry under one of the greatest teachers I ever had, Lily Stafford, who taught many boys who later became physicians.

I carried a heavy course load my junior year, but I still had one burning desire: to letter in football at Lawton High and be given a big red sweater with a big white "L" on it. Every day I wore clean bib overalls for lack of a better uniform, and I felt that a big red sweater with a big white "L" would make me into an outstanding boy.

During the first four games, I got in about one quarter in each game. And then came the big game with Ardmore, Oklahoma, which was to be played in Ardmore. That week I worked hard and prayed hard. On Thursday night I had an encounter with the Lord. I wanted desperately to make that road trip to Ardmore with the football team, but that night I

*Lawton High School basketball team in late 1920s, left to right: Jess Ferrell, Charles Green, Nim Newberry, Jack Reese, Cash Gentry, E. B. Dunlop, Glen Bolton, Raoul Valdez, and Coach Ray Norton.*

received a message—I do not know whether it was a dream or what—that my name would not be on the travel squad, but that I would be able to play enough football to letter that year.

When I awakened the next morning, my mother had a wonderful breakfast, but I could not eat very much. I ran all the way to high school, and went down in the basement to Coach Bryan Griffin's room, and looked over the list of the travel squad; sure enough, my name was not on it.

The team went to Ardmore without me, and they lost the game. On Monday afternoon in practice, Coach Griff changed the whole lineup. He moved some of us second-team boys up to first team, and I started the game the next week as a center. Then I started every game the rest of the year. I received a varsity sweater and letter.

On the day of the assembly when the football players were to be honored and given their big red sweaters with the big white "L" on it, I was in the chemistry lab under the supervision of my teacher, Lily Stafford. We were filtering out sulfide, and I was so anxious to get down to assembly that I left in the middle of my experiment. I rushed to the auditorium to get in line to get my sweater, and after I received it, I put it on and felt twice as big.

I rushed back up to the lab to see what was happening. Miss Stafford was standing at my experiment and said, "Charles Green, you almost burned up my lab. Don't you know that litmus paper, when it becomes dry, will ignite?" I said, "Miss Stafford, I'm sorry. I was anxious to get my first red sweater." She said, "Well, you football players are the poorest students." Then and there, I decided I had better be a better student in chemistry if I planned to become a physician.

In my senior year in 1929, I was a regular on the football team. I had won my position. I had been able to keep my grade average above ninety. Our class met in the auditorium one morning to elect the president of the senior class. W. J. Becker and Miss Ora Gentry were our class sponsors. Bob Randolph had been president of our class for three years, and everyone knew that he wanted to be the president of the senior class. However, out of the clear blue sky, Faye Hillis, who played left guard on the football team, got up and nominated me for the presidency. Bob Randolph was also nominated. W. J. Becker asked the two of us to go out into the hall while the students voted. I felt unqualified and told Bob Randolph that I hoped I would not be elected. When we returned to the auditorium, Becker announced that I had won the presidency of the senior class. I do not remember exactly what I said, but I told the students and faculty that I was overwhelmed, that I was grateful, and that I would do the best job possible.

My senior year was a wonderful year. I presided at the junior-senior banquet. I had a date with Margaret Belle Godlove, which was one of the few dates I had that year.

On the night of graduation in May 1930, I received the American Legion Award for the best all-around boy, and Miss Lily Stafford presented me with the McClure Medal for the highest grade in chemistry. She gave me a smile when I walked up on stage that night at graduation. I have always felt that she was a great Christian woman and a wonderful teacher.

That night was a beautiful moon-lit night, and Fred Hammond, a classmate, and Maurice Meyer and I walked home. Fred announced that he was going to become a physician. His father was one of the pioneer physicians in Lawton, and I announced to him that I also hoped to be a doctor. Maurice informed us his dad was a mechanic and that he was going to be a Ford mechanic. That night we all looked up at the moon, and Fred said, "We can almost see a man in the moon tonight." Little did we dream that many, many years later, in 1969, a man would be walking on the moon.

# CHAPTER 4

# College and University Experiences

IN 1930, AT THE START OF THE GREAT DEPRESSION, I was having some difficulty trying to find a place to go to college to pursue my premedical work.

That spring, I was able to secure employment at the Fairmont Creamery and worked in the office of Mr. Patten, the president of the company. I picked up the mail and was an "errand boy" for several of his staff.

In May I received a telephone call that my father had come back to Oklahoma and was in Oklahoma City and wanted to see me. He was staying at a hotel on Reno Street where all the oil-field workers hung out. I went to Oklahoma City and spent two days and nights with my father, the first time that I had seen him in several years. He informed me that he was proud of my high school record and was sorry that he had never been able to see me play football.

The night we were together, we attended a big tent revival on a vacant lot on Reno Street. That was the only time I ever saw my father in a church service. The next morning he went on to Olathe, Kansas, to begin work, and I returned to Lawton.

One week later, we received word that my father had been killed in an oil-field accident. My mother had remarried an old bachelor by the name of Sergeant William Brooks. He called me by telephone at the Fairmont Creamery where I was working and said, "Bud, hurry home, we have some tragic news." He did not tell me what had happened. I left the Fairmont Creamery Station and ran all the way home on Third Street. When I arrived home, my sisters were crying. My stepfather showed me the telegram that my father had been killed. That was on Friday.

On Sunday my pastor, Brother T. B. Holcomb, and Pete Monroe, the undertaker for the Ritter Funeral Home, went with me to the Frisco Railway Station, where my father's casket was to arrive at 4:00 P.M. I rode in the car with Brother Holcomb and Pete Monroe back to the funeral home. When they opened the casket, I was hoping that it was not my dad, but it was. I was grateful that I had had one night with him before he was killed.

Then I thought that my hopes were blasted, that I would never become a physician without a dad to help me, to support me. His financial contributions had been few and of little significance in the past, but as long as he was alive, there was always hope.

My first year in Cameron College, in 1930-1931, was filled with excitement and apprehension. My college chemistry professor for two years was Clarence Breedlove, whom all of us called "Doc" Breedlove. He helped me secure my premedical prerequisites. My English teacher was Ruth Malcom. I had to have two years of foreign language, and I chose German. My teacher was Mrs. Winchel Barber, the wife of the president of the American National Bank in Lawton. My math teacher was Mrs. Cavanaugh, and she taught me college algebra and trigonometry.

During my first year in Cameron, several students formed a premedical group: Wilbur Lewis, Howard Angus, Emry Agee, Doss Lynn, Wilbur Bohlman, and myself. At the end of my first semester, John Coffey, the president of Cameron, announced that several of us had a grade average above ninety. Thus, we were initiated into Phi Theta Kappa, the honorary fraternity of

Cameron College. During my second semester, I was elected president of the Phi Theta Kappa fraternity for the year 1931-32. Forest Brown, a premedical student, and I were elected delegates to attend the national convention of Phi Theta Kappa in Weatherford, Texas. At that time, there was a junior college in Weatherford which hosted the Phi Theta Kappa convention.

In the spring of 1931, Forest Brown and I decided to attend the convention, but we had no transportation. The local chapter collected twelve dollars. We went to the Chevrolet agency and talked to Cecil Green. He let us have a second-hand Ford roadster, with no top on it, and he gave us a tank of gasoline.

We started one Saturday afternoon toward Weatherford, Texas. We got to Wichita Falls, Texas, about dark, ate a hamburger, and headed to Fort Worth. When we got within ten or fifteen miles of the city, it practically lit up the sky. It seemed like we had driven half the night. We did not get to Fort Worth until about two o'clock in the morning. We stopped and parked in front of a downtown hotel. When we tried to get a room, the clerk informed us there were no rooms available, but he also told us that he would let us sleep on a couple of divans in the hotel lobby. The next morning we ate breakfast in the hotel, thanked the clerk for giving us a place to lodge, and started for Weatherford, which was only a few miles from Fort Worth.

We arrived at the Weatherford Junior College about eleven o'clock in the morning. We were assigned a room in the home of a lawyer named Grindstaff. He had a beautiful new house. Forest Brown and I had the privilege of enjoying the accommodation of this beautiful home and the wonderful generosity of this young lawyer and his wife.

At the convention, Forest nominated me as vice-president of the national organization of Phi Theta Kappa, and I was elected. We returned to Cameron Junior College on Wednesday, and on Thursday morning at a special assembly, I was honored as being the national vice-president of Phi Theta Kappa.

That year I also decided I would run for president of the student senate. My campaign manager was Lucille Carter. I was elected president of the student senate for the year 1931-1932.

We all met at Lucille's parents' sandwich and hamburger shop and had a celebration.

During the summer of 1931, I worked at the Fairmont Creamery. Every Sunday morning, at four o'clock, I and the others lucky enough to have a job reported to work dumping cream in the big vat in the butter room. In those days the farmers would bring their eggs and cream into the cream stations in little towns like Chattanooga, Randlett, and Faxon. Then they would be trucked into the Fairmont Creamery, arriving between midnight and 4:00 A.M.

When school opened my sophomore year at Cameron, in the fall of 1931, I decided to play football. I played in practically every game as a second-team center under a great coach, Penn O. Dickson. Also that year I served as president of Phi Theta Kappa and of the student senate.

I enrolled in calculus my sophomore year but stayed in that class only one week. I informed Mrs. Cavanaugh, my teacher, that I was not going to become an engineer; she said I would not need calculus, so I dropped that class. Calculus was beyond me. I am glad I decided to be a doctor instead of an engineer.

In January 1932 we were in the Great Depression, and Mr. Patten, the head of the Fairmont Creamery, called all the Cameron students into his office and told us that he would have to terminate our work because the creamery had to tighten its belt. When the second semester opened at Cameron, I had no money to enroll, and the banks were even failing.

My mother told me to go and tell the registrar, Mr. Elkins, that I had no money. I told him my story, and I will never forget what he did for me. He said, "Charles, I will take your enrollment form and put it in my desk and give you a slip to take to all of your classes this second semester. Tell your teachers that you are paid in full, and next summer when you get a job, you come out and pay me the five dollars." We had a gentlemen's agreement. Only five dollars stood between me and an M.D. I assured him I would pay him.

I went ahead and finished my premedical work with a grade point average of ninety-two. During the summer months I cut grass and made enough money to pay Mr. Elkins and completed my assignment at Cameron Junior College. This was my first big hurdle.

That summer Wilbur Lewis invited me to go on a trip with him, Emry Agee, Doss Lynn, and Wilbur Bohlman—all premedical students. We were searching for a school to help us complete our premedical work, from which we could then apply for admission to a medical school. Wilbur had a car and took us all to Fayetteville, Arkansas, during the first week of September 1932 to explore the possibility of going to the University of Arkansas. I had been able to get money from the Rotary Scholarship Fund. And Winchel Barber, president of the bank, had let me have fifty dollars, so I had available that money to enroll for college for my junior year. We rented a large house in Fayetteville and lived on apples and concord grapes. We bought other food at a nearby market.

On my first day there, I went to the athletic department and decided to go out for football. The freshman coach, a former All-American end for the Razorbacks, gave me the equipment, and the next day I went out for practice. He informed me that since I was an out-of-state student, I would have to tell a lie. He asked me to say that I was from Arkansas. He said, "Do you have any folks in Arkansas?" I said, "Yes, my mother's folks, the Pendletons, came from Fort Smith." He said, "Well, tell them Fort Smith is your home." That night I did not sleep well. I knew that if I told them I was from Fort Smith and they checked and discovered I was from Lawton, I might get kicked out of the university, and that might jeopardize all my chances to be a physician and realize my dream.

So the next morning I checked in all of my equipment and told the coach I was going back to Oklahoma. Then I had to tell my dear friends, Wilbur Lewis, Emry Agee, Wilbur Bohlman, and Doss Lynn, that I would be leaving. They took me out to the highway that morning, and I hitchhiked from Fayetteville, Arkansas, to Norman, Oklahoma. I walked the streets of the University of Oklahoma at Norman and tried to find work, but nothing was available. My options seemed limited.

I went home and told my mother that my school days were over, and that I would have to find employment. The next afternoon I was sitting on the front porch at 707 F Street looking at the want ads in the *Lawton Constitution* to see if I could find a job. About four o'clock in the afternoon, my mother came out to the porch and said, "Bud, there is somebody on the phone from Norman. His name is Tom Munson. He wants to talk to you." I said, "That's one of my high school friends. Tom was a year ahead of me in Lawton High."

I went to the phone, and Tom said, "Charles, I heard you were in Norman a few days ago looking for a job to go to school and you didn't find any." I said, "That's right." He said, "I have a job for you. I live in a small house in the back of a boardinghouse. The boy who was to work here and wait tables had a major operation and cannot return. Would you like to have the job?" I assured Tom that the next morning I would be on the highway hitchhiking to Norman.

The next day I arrived in Norman about ten o'clock and went to the boardinghouse. Nora Wells operated it. Tom Munson was waiting there. I got the job. Tom and I became roommates in a little house in the back of the boardinghouse. We did not have a bathroom. We had to go into the big boardinghouse and use their bathroom and take showers. That whole year I had the privilege of going to Oklahoma University, and I feel God Almighty worked through Tom Munson to help me get to the campus.

Mrs. Wells had me get up early Sunday morning and make homemade ice cream. We had it all during the winter months. She was a wonderful lady. I got my meals, and all it cost me to room with Tom Munson in that small house was five dollars a month.

That year I was able to work with Earl Sneed, the business manager of the yearbook, and helped with the circulation of the yearbooks. There were four thousand students, but no one had any money. Since it was 1932-1933, the deep part of the Great Depression, we sold the yearbooks for a dollar down and a dollar per month. I received a special permit, and identification card to visit every sorority and every fraternity on the campus each month and collect a dollar for each yearbook.

In those cold winter months, I had only a jacket and a big red "L" sweater. I went to all the fraternities on the northeast corner of the campus. Around eleven o'clock, those girls were wonderful. They would have some hot chocolate for me. I had a secretary in each sorority, and she would get the money and would write the receipts. I would get back home to the little house behind the boardinghouse about midnight. That enabled me to stay in school.

That was the first year I voted, and I voted for Franklin D. Roosevelt. My English teacher was Mrs. Jewel Wurtzbaugh. She was one of the best teachers I ever had in English. Also that year, I joined the First Baptist Church of Norman and came under the leadership of Ed Hallock, one of the greatest Christians I ever knew. He served as pastor of the church and was a great friend of all Oklahoma University students. During the spring semester, I decided to enter the ministry and shared my decision with him. He asked me to be a Sunday School teacher of twelve-year-old boys in the Junior Sunday School department. Every Sunday night after church, a group of us would go to Brother Hallock's home for peanut butter and jelly sandwiches and milk. That group evolved into the first Baptist Student Union on campus.

I met many wonderful people that year. Leslie Paine later became a lawyer in Anadarko. O. T. McCall became an outstanding businessman in Norman. I dated Mary Lou Parker and liked her very much. I told her that I was definitely going into the ministry and would like to write her and carry on a correspondence because she graduated that spring. I received a "Dear John" letter from her one day saying that she had not told me that her father was a Methodist preacher and that her mother had decided that her daughter was not going to marry a Baptist preacher.

That spring I became a part of a preacher's team, which included both a Presbyterian preacher and an Episcopal preacher. Dr. Comfort, the head of the School of Religion at Oklahoma University, had us to go out every Sunday morning and preach at the mental hospital in Norman. The patients would come to a large auditorium, and we had one sermon, the Prodigal son. Each of us took a part. I had the part of the Father, and I had the opportunity to present the love of a Heavenly Father, how he welcomed his boy back home.

Every Sunday when we finished, the patients would come by, and one dear lady would always say, "Brother Green, that's the greatest sermon I ever heard." She might have been a mental patient, but she made me feel good.

That spring Robert Hughes, the associational missionary, decided that I could help him by preaching all that summer at little country churches that had fallen by the wayside and by trying to revive them; I promised him I would do it. I had no sermons, but Ed Hallock gave me some old ones. One day in June at Hallock's home, Hughes picked me up and took me about eight miles east of Norman to an old schoolhouse, where he said I was to be their preacher. I asked him, "Where are the other members of the team to help me?" He said, "You are the team. You are it." So he deposited me on the steps of this little one-room schoolhouse, and left me sitting there.

When darkness came, about four families showed up. They had no key to the building, and we did not have any light. We had a prayer meeting on the steps that night. After the benediction, one of the families came by and said, "Brother Green, we don't have a room for you, but you can sleep in Grandpa's room on a pallet on the floor." That was where I stayed that whole week. They took me home with them. They made me a pallet in front of the screen door. And it was air conditioned because there were big holes in the screen door. Grandpa snored all night, so I did not get much sleep.

I preached all week in that little schoolhouse and did not have any visible results. When the collection was taken, I was given eighty-nine cents. (Later on, I would tell this story to my Sunday School class at the First Baptist Church of Lawton, and one of my dearest friends, Doc Ramey, would say, "Doctor Green, you were overpaid for one week of service.") I got board and room. I ate fried chicken and okra. They washed my shirt every night, and it was dry and clean the next morning. Bob

Hughes picked me up Sunday night and took me back to Norman, and I hitchhiked the next morning back to Lawton.

For the next assignment, I want to Mount Zion Church near Lindsay, Oklahoma, and worked for two weeks in a revival with Don Thrasher, a young preacher. I lived with a dear, old couple who had no children, but they had a bedroom, a preacher's room, for me. Each morning I would go to the First Baptist Church of Lindsay, where Brother Cherry was pastor, and hear Dr. E. C. Routh. While conducting a revival there, he had both a morning Bible hour and a prayer hour. Dr. Routh became a dear friend. His son, Porter Routh, became a classmate of mine at Oklahoma Baptist University, and we graduated together. Years later, my son, Larry, married his daughter, Betsy, and we shared three grandchildren.

After that revival I returned to Lawton, and Brother Holcomb, my pastor, arranged to have a youth revival on the Emerson School grounds, which were just across the street from the First Baptist Church. We secured a large tent, and Brother Holcomb let us have some wooden benches from the church; we held a week-long revival. We had hardly any visible results, but we felt that everyone got somewhat revived. At least, we hoped.

For my senior year, Brother Holcomb felt that I should go to Oklahoma Baptist University. He assured me that the Woman's Missionary Union would help me and that missionary students would get half of their tuition paid by the Oklahoma Baptist Convention. So I enrolled in the fall of 1933 at OBU as a senior student. I also went out for football and played second-team center. I made all the trips but did not get enough quarters for a varsity letter.

OBU became a key part of my whole life. I became friends of many boys who became leaders in Southern Baptist work. I roomed with about seven other preacher men who were to become music directors of Baptist churches. My roommates were Truett and Darwin Farmer, Alvida Harrison, Jesse Northcutt, Carl Mabre, and Max Stanfield.

While at OBU I was called in January 1934 to the Bearden Baptist Church. Having been called to a church enabled me to be ordained by the First Baptist Church in Lawton, and Brother Holcomb arranged to have W. A. Wilcoxson preach my ordination ceremony. Brother Earl Stark, pastor of the Central Baptist Church, gave the charge. I remember that night as they questioned me; they asked me if I believed every word of the Bible. And I told them I did. They asked me if I would tithe. I said I already did. As a full-time pastor, I went every Sunday to Bearden, Oklahoma, along with another young minister, Dan Beltz. He had a car, dropped me off at Bearden each weekend, and picked me up on Sunday night; I earned five dollars a Sunday. That year about six of us lived upstairs in a big boardinghouse. We cooked our own meals.

In the spring of 1934, OBU let the students be the professors and the president for one day. We had a day in assembly. I was selected to be the president of OBU that day in place of Hale V. Davis. I went to the home of Davis and his wife; she, a dear lady, let me borrow a suit. It was a beautiful gray suit, and fortunately it was my size. She also loaned me a tie and shirt. That morning in chapel I was the president of OBU. I told them that right in the middle of the Great Depression, we were all hopefully going to graduate. As president of the university, I declared a holiday that day, and the whole student body stood up and gave me a standing ovation.

That same spring, I went over to the Oklahoma University School of Medicine and met with the dean of the medical school. He told me that there was very little opportunity for me to be accepted as a first-year student. I had all the academic requirements, but I had no money. So he told me there was no need to apply. I returned to Oklahoma Baptist University and went with a group to my first Southern Baptist Convention, in May 1934. Dr. Fred Watts, an OBU professor, gave us a trip to the SBC meeting in Fort Worth, Texas, in the big coliseum near the stockyards. Alvida Harrison, Dan Beltz, Carl Mabre, and I went with him. We were all seniors. We all four stayed in the basement of a Baptist church, which had cots for the students. We slept on cots and had enough money to live on hamburgers. The most important sermon was given by Dr. George W. Truett, pastor of the First Baptist Church at Dallas. He had just returned from London, where he had spoken on the one hundredth anniversary of Charles Haddon Spurgeon's birth.

Dr. Truett gave us such a wonderful message. And right in that service I decided I wanted to give my life, somewhere, somehow, completely to the Lord, either as a medical missionary or as a minister.

Dr. Watts also took us out to Seminary Hill, which was the home of the Southwestern Baptist Theological Seminary. At that time, there were only a few buildings on a hill, with no shrubs or trees, and it looked rather barren; but I thought, "Well, this is where I will spend my next three years."

We returned to the campus at Oklahoma Baptist University for my last month of college work. One day a fellow by the name of George A. Ritchey came to our campus. He had come all the way from Louisville, Kentucky, from the Southern Baptist Theological Seminary to recruit Oklahoma students to come to that seminary. He said, "We only have two Oklahoma boys, Leonard Stigler and Eugene Hill, and we would like to extend an invitation and full three-year scholarships to three of the seniors this year at Oklahoma Baptist University." Alvida Harrison, Dan Beltz, and I became the three recipients.

In September 1934 Bearden Baptist Church took an offering and gave me fourteen dollars to pay my bus fare to Louisville. Also at my home at 707 F, several of my friends, Maurice Meyer, James Lawrence, Howard Troop, Russell Marshall, and Edith May Best, came to bid me farewell. We had a little party in my home. My sister invited one of her classmates, Jennie Sullivan, to come; I barely met her that night, but she would later become my wife. But that night my eyes were on Edith May Best, who had been our football queen, a little petite lady with a beautiful smile and beautiful eyes.

The next day I caught a Greyhound bus for Louisville. I changed buses in Oklahoma City and Tulsa and arrived in Joplin, Missouri, about midnight. I changed buses again and rode all night to St. Louis, arriving there the next morning. After a layover, I caught a bus for Louisville that afternoon about 1:30 and arrived in Louisville about 7:00 P.M.

The Greyhound bus station was on Broadway, and I asked a ticket agent how to get to the seminary. He told me I would have to go one block to Chestnut Street, catch a streetcar going straight east, get off at Crescent Hill Baptist Church, and go south another block. At the next street, there would be a streetlight and a pathway. I would follow that pathway right to the seminary. I followed those directions right to Mullins Hall, which was the dormitory for the single students.

Arriving at ten o'clock at night, I was bone tired and hungry. The fellow who met me there informed me that he would give me a room, but there were no linens or blankets; the mattress did have a covering on it. He assigned me a room, and by eleven o'clock that night I unpacked and was asleep.

The next morning I awakened on the campus of the seminary and looked across to Norton Hall, and saw beautiful green grass. Oklahoma had been dry; we had had a severe drought. This was like heaven. I opened my door on Sunday morning and soon met a young fellow by the name of Wilfred Congdon, who would later become a missionary to Africa. He told me an unbelievable story. He had ridden all the way from his home in Colorado to Louisville on a bicycle. Since Wilfred and I were informed that the dining hall would not open until Monday night, we pooled our money and bought a loaf of bread, a quart of milk, and some bologna. We lived on bologna sandwiches Sunday and Monday. On Monday we enrolled in the seminary as first-year students. I received my permanent room assignment. My first meal in the seminary included grits, something I had never eaten, but they were good. Those southern boys from South Carolina, North Carolina, Alabama, and Georgia ate grits like they were strawberry cake. We had a good meal, and the next day I was a student in the Southern Baptist Theological Seminary. Exciting days lay ahead.

# CHAPTER 5

# Southern Baptist Theological Seminary

MY FIRST YEAR AT THE SOUTHERN BAPTIST Theological Seminary, beginning in the fall of 1934, was wonderful. Dr. Hershey Davis taught my first class—New Testament. He was one of the greatest Bible teachers I had in my seminary days.

I had Dr. W. O. Carver in missions and Dr. J. B. Weatherspoon in homiletics. I recited only one time under Dr. A. T. Robertson, the great Greek teacher. He asked me that morning, when he called my name to recite, if I had ever preached from the Apocrypha. I said, "I didn't even know that was in the Bible." He said, "I won't grade you this morning." Later, I discovered that it was material produced between the Old and New Testament eras and that the Catholic Church used it frequently.

I remember that when we would have the assembly every morning, Dr. Robertson would go around to the windows and open them. He said when he died he was going to leave enough money in a trust fund to have a sexton who could help regulate the temperature. Dr. Robertson died from a stroke the second week of school. When he died, I attended the funeral of this great teacher.

There were several hundred students in Dr. Davis's New Testament class, with two to a seat; I sat by Pete Gillespie from Illinois, who later became a missionary to Japan. Pete became a dear friend. The first year I was in the seminary, I did not have any church work, and he and I would go with a group every Saturday night and preach on the streets of Louisville in front of a saloon. One night the owner of the saloon rolled out a whiskey barrel and said, "Get up on top of the whiskey barrel and you can do a better job." And I did.

When the winter days came, Pete and I went with a group to the Bowery Mission, located in the basement of an old abandoned building. Seminary mess hall furnished hot coffee and sandwiches, and we preached to all the homeless men. Forty to fifty men would come in and sit on benches in that basement.

We made a mistake the first time we preached at the mission. We fed them coffee and sandwiches first; then, when Pete and I got up to preach, the men had left. So the next Saturday night we saved the sandwiches and coffee until after the sermon, and they all stayed; we had a captive audience.

Most of these men had been alcoholics or mental cases and lost their families, and they came there for some warm coffee and a sandwich. They were hungry, and also hungry to hear the gospel. They were needy, and I know that God loved them.

On Sunday mornings Pete Gillespie and I took an old seminary bus to Waverly Hills TB Sanitarium, located several miles west of Louisville. In those days the TB patients slept and lived on a large screen porch. At least a hundred occupied a long screen porch on the second floor. When the cold days came, I preached in an overcoat. The Sunday before Christmas, one of the patients asked me to stop at her bed. She pulled out a beautiful Christmas-wrapped present, a big one. It had shaving cream, aftershave lotion, and a razor with some extra blades.

About ten o'clock, we rode the old seminary bus to one of the churches for the eleven o'clock service. I remember going to Highland Baptist Church and hearing Dr. Brown, and to Walnut

Street Church where Dr. Gibson preached.

During the second semester, I informed my friends that I would have to leave the seminary. My stepfather had died, and my mother was receiving a small pension of seventy-five dollars a month since he had been a veteran of the Spanish-American War. At the end of the school year, I would return to Lawton and find a job. Just before the school year ended, George Ritchey, who had invited me to come to the seminary and had extended the scholarship invitation, came to my room and said, "Charles, I understand you are going to leave the school because you have run out of money." I said, "That's right." He said, "Well, I want you to go with me to Paragon, Indiana. I'm finishing my work. I have finished my education here. I have received my Ph.D., and I have been called as pastor of the First Baptist Church of Lafayette, Indiana. The last Sunday in May I want you to go with me and try out at my churches." I accepted the invitation.

The last Sunday in May, I went with George to Paragon and preached for him at Paragon, a half-time church, at New Salem, a quarter-time church, and at Samaria, a quarter-time church. George then took me back to the seminary.

On Monday morning, Leonard Stigler, a friend from Oklahoma, took me out on the highway to hitchhike to Lawton, Oklahoma. I was able to reach St. Louis about dark. I only had about sixty cents in my pocket, but I had met a young lady at the Carver Training School by the name of Flontine Walker. She said if I came through St. Louis, she would be working that summer for her uncle, who was pastor of the King's Highway Baptist Church. So when I got into St. Louis, I called her and she told me what streetcar to catch. They lived way out in the west part of St. Louis. I caught a streetcar, and they met me. That night they gave me supper in their small parsonage. I slept with the pastor.

The next morning, after a wonderful breakfast, the pastor took me out to Highway 66 in St. Louis, and I hitchhiked as far as Joplin, Missouri. There I called a friend who was in the seminary with me. He picked me up, and I spent the night, sleeping with two of his brothers. The next morning, I ate breakfast with

*Seminary students drive to Paragon, Indiana, for a missionary conference, left to right: Charles E. Green, Oklahoma; C. K. Djang, China; Sadamoto Kawano, Japan; and Clayton Waddell, Alabama.*

him, and he took me to Highway 66 on the west side of Joplin. I reached Lawton that night.

My mother told me that the deacons of the Calvary Baptist Church were trying to locate me. Brother W. A. Wilcoxson had undergone major surgery and wanted to rest the whole month of June. So he invited me to preach the whole month of June at the Calvary Baptist Church. That was a wonderful opportunity. The church met in a large wooden tabernacle at 7th and H. It was a warm, loving church, and Brother Wilcoxson was a loving pastor who cared for his people. That association was a great, positive force in my life.

The first week I was there we held a Vacation Bible School with over three hundred enrolled. Each morning when we would assemble to go in, a young lady, Jennie Sullivan, who lived about half a block west of the church, stopped by. I had friendly chats with her. She worked as a secretary for the Prudential Insurance Company. I had become acquainted with her when I met her at my going-away party the year before. We became friends, and when I had occasion to date her, we would share a nickel's worth of popcorn and a coke. We developed a wonderful relationship and the beginning of a wonderful romance.

At the end of June I received a letter from the clerk of the First Baptist Church of Paragon, Indiana, saying that I had been called as pastor of that church and of two rural churches in Salem, south of Paragon, and Samaria, west of Paragon. The last Sunday in June, I preached for Brother Wilcoxson at the Calvary Baptist Church in Lawton, and he had recovered sufficiently to resume his work as the pastor. I took a bus to Martinsville, Indiana, and some of the people at Paragon met me and took me out to Paragon. I stayed in the home of Dr. and Mrs. McNeil. This was a wonderful experience because they were among the few people in Paragon who had an indoor bathroom, and I could take a shower every night.

On the first Sunday, July 4, 1935, I was to go to New Salem. I had to cross the White River, and there had been a heavy rain. So the river was up. That morning I only had about eighteen in Sunday School. Many members worried about the river getting over the corn, which was only about a foot high. Fortunately, the river receded, and the corn crop was saved.

The next Sunday at New Salem, we had a large crowd of about forty or fifty people. One dear lady asked me to go home with her. She said her husband, Charles Whitesell, was sick. He was dying of tuberculosis, and he was not a Christian. I told her that I had already been booked that Sunday to go with a family who had prepared Sunday dinner. I then promised her that, "The next Sunday I'm here, I will go with you." That would be in September.

At Paragon I preached two Sundays every month. I received twenty dollars each Sunday. At the country churches, I received fifteen dollars a Sunday. At Whitaker, a little village west of Paragon, with one store and a saw mill, I preached every fifth Sunday. So I received about ninety dollars a month for preaching. I gave my tithe, and I sent my mother eight dollars every week to help her. The Lord took care of me.

*Vacation Bible School at Paragon Baptist Church in May 1936, with Charles Green, pastor, eighth from left on back row.*

While pastor of these churches, each had a family with a preacher's room. Many times I stayed with Charlie and Aunt Alice Dow at Samaria. They had two children, Bessie and Harry. Then at New Salem, I stayed in the home of the Charles Bakers. They had two children a little younger than I, Herschel and Mary. At Paragon Aunt Alice Whitaker, a childless widow who was advanced in years, had a beautiful home. She gave me the front room, a big room, which had a big featherbed in it. That became my home during my days at Paragon.

Aunt Alice Whitaker and Attie Asher, who had also lost her husband, lived at Samaria and became two of my dearest friends. They counseled me. At times, when I was short of money, Attie Asher would loan me five dollars, and I would pay her back. Aunt Alice gave me some wonderful meals and a place to enjoy and study. I performed a marriage ceremony in her house for Harold Schaly, a classmate of mine from Brazil, and Mildred Hopwood, whom I had introduced to him during a young people's retreat at McCormick State Park. They became missionaries and are still in Brazil.

I was awakened early one morning in Aunt Alice Whitaker's home by Blan Applegate, who lived next door with his father. He said, "Brother Green, I want you to marry me and Janice Cherry." I said, "Well, I've got to get back to the seminary Monday. I have to be in class Tuesday." He said, "Well, after you marry us, we will take you to Louisville." That was the deal.

That was my first couple to marry in Paragon. Every time I go back for a reunion, I always see Blan Applegate and Janice Cherry, who have been married over fifty years.

During my third year at the seminary, a committee selected me to be chairman of Mullins Hall, the single men's dorm. We ran a little concession store. The boys would study Greek and Hebrew and come at night for sandwiches and cold drinks. We had a pickup for dry cleaning and laundry, and we had a barber shop run by Kent Pendergraff. All of this was a big responsibility. We made a little money and used it to help other students.

I had a whole year to finish postgraduate work at the seminary, and I enrolled under Dr. Hershey Davis for a year of study in New Testament. And in that class were Herschel Hobbs, W. A. Criswell, and Claud Bowen. Hobbs and Criswell would later serve as presidents of the Southern Baptist Convention. Herschel and Frances Hobbs lived in Rice Hall, which was for married couples at the seminary. When Herschel came over to the barbershop to get a haircut, the word would get around that he was there telling some of his latest jokes and stories. We would gather in the doorway of the barbershop to listen to this fellow. We would all welcome him when he came to Mullins Hall because he left us with a merry heart.

CHAPTER 6

# Indiana University Medical School

BEFORE I RECEIVED MY MASTER OF THEOLOGY degree in 1937, I woke up and I said, "Well, here is the Indiana University Medical School only forty miles from Paragon." So I decided to have my transcripts sent there to see if I could be admitted. First, I had to get an appointment with the Admissions Committee. In the spring of 1938, I went down to Bloomington, Indiana, where the first year of medical school was located. I met with Dr. John Hill, Dr. Meyers the dean, and one of the other professors. They quizzed me about why I was leaving the ministry and going into medicine. I shared with them that I wanted to be a medical missionary. They informed me that the new class was one of the brightest classes ever admitted to Indiana University, that I had only a 3.4 average, that it had been four years since I had had my pre-medical work, and that I might have a difficult time. I assured them that I would like to have a chance.

I went back to Paragon and prayed and waited patiently. I received a letter in June 1938 saying that I had been admitted as a freshman to the Indiana University School of Medicine;

enrollment would take place in September. The letter also said, "Send ten dollars to hold your place." I did not have the ten dollars. I received a second letter saying, "We have not received your ten dollars. If you do not let us know, we will have to give your place to an alternate." I went to the Paragon State Bank and talked to Mr. R. E. Hendrickson, who was both bank president and a member of my church. The bank loaned me ten dollars. I assured Hendrickson that when I held my next revival, I would pay him back, and I did. I sent the ten dollars to the medical school.

In September 1938, I had an old Model A Ford car, a 1929 model, which I drove to Bloomington for my first year in medicine. They were calling the roll for the year in the amphitheater of the new medical building. When the speaker called my name, I sat there a while and thought, "Well, that's me." I have waited six years for this medical school. Finally, he said, "Is Charles Green here?" I said, "Yes, sir." I walked down some rather dark steps and found my seat next to Harrison Green and George Godersky. That first day the first fellow who came over to meet me said, "I'm Joe Smith and my dad is a Christian minister and I want to welcome you to our class."

When we were assigned our cadavers in the gross anatomy lab, I was assigned to three young men I had never met: Joe Buchmeier, Al Ritz, and Andy Hampshire. They were all Catholics. Joe Buchmeier became my partner, a wonderful friend, and later he wanted to be married. He was the first of eighteen classmates whom I would marry. He said, "I'm a Catholic, but I've fallen in love with a little Presbyterian nurse, and I want to marry her. I've cleared it with the priest here in Bloomington, and I want you to perform our ceremony in her home in Martinsville, Indiana." And I did.

That year was a wonderful year. Everybody was friendly, and they nicknamed me "Rev.," sometimes "Rev. Green." I was the only preacher in my class out of 129 students. Dr. Ross, the professor in that class, would come by every Monday morning and call me "Sky Pilot." He would say, "Sky Pilot, how was the collection this week?" I would say, "Very good. I got enough money. I'm still in school." He would say, "That's great."

The first semester rolled by, and the names of those who had made their grades and could continue their second semester were posted on the window of the gross anatomy class. I went down the list and found my name. I had an eighty-eight average. About eight of our class either failed or left for some other reason.

The second semester started in January, and that month was one of the coldest, with the heaviest snowfall, that Paragon had experienced. My church people had a lot of sickness, including a flu epidemic. Instead of having eighty and ninety in Sunday School, we had around twelve or fourteen for several Sundays. The collections amounted to only about two dollars a Sunday. I was to get twenty dollars at Paragon but received only two, and I could not pay my tuition bill. During the last week in January, the secretary of Dean Meyers of the medical school found me and asked, "Are you Charles Green?" I said, "Yes." She said, "Well, the dean wants to see you immediately in his office." Everybody around me heard what she said. I dropped my scalpel.

When I went that morning to see the dean, he had a long list. He said, "I have a list here of delinquent students who haven't paid their tuition. Your name is the only name of 450 students in IU Medical School. You're the only one who hasn't paid your tuition." I said, "That's right. My church has been in the grip of a flu epidemic. Snow has been on the ground. Our attendance has been very small. Our collections have been only about two dollars a Sunday. Dr. Meyers, I just don't have any money." He said, "I remember. I was on the Admissions Committee, and you told us you were a preacher and your dad was dead and you had no money. You know the rules of Indiana University. If you don't pay the registrar next week, I will have to drop you." I assured him that I would try to have the money.

I left the dean's office and went back into the gross anatomy lab. All my classmates came around and said, "Rev., be honest with us and tell us what has happened. We know you have made your grades. What has happened?" I said, "Well, I've run out of money. I don't have money to pay my tuition. I'm going to have to drop out." They said, "Rev., we're going to take an offering here. We've got over a hundred students. It will take 140 dollars, and we're going to raise the money." I said, "No, I came to medical school by faith, and I know the Lord will take care of me." They said, "Well, that's for the birds. You have to have money on the barrelhead here if you're going to stay in school." I said, "Yes, but the Lord will provide."

That weekend I went out to Paragon. Snow was still on the ground. I went to the basement of the church building. Brother Suter was the janitor, and I had won him to Christ on the liars' bench by the barbershop one Sunday morning, and I had baptized him in White River. He was building a fire and said, "Brother Green, there won't be many people here this morning." Sure enough, only about sixteen people came. I went around all Sunday afternoon in the snow and prayed with people who had the flu.

On Sunday night I visited the home of Helena Randall, as I usually did on Sunday evenings, when her mother would give me chess pie, a cup of coffee, and a check. She and her mother lived in a little house on the edge of Paragon. She was the postmaster of that little town. She was also the treasurer of the church, but she had not come to church that morning. The mother came to the door and said, "Come on in. We have some good news for you." I said, "Praise the Lord, that's the first time I have heard something about good news. I want to know what it is." She said, "Well, sit down. I've got the pie and the coffee ready, and when you finish I will take you back to the bedroom, and we will sit down and talk to Helena. She wants to tell you the story."

I ate the pie and drank my coffee, and her mother took me back to the bedroom. I sat down next to the bed, and Helena said, "I want to tell you a wonderful story. You know last summer one of our schoolteachers, a member of our church, Esther Potter, got married and you performed the ceremony." She had married a big Canadian boy, Harry Baade, from Imperial Saskatchewan. She said, "Last week they wrote me and sent me a check for $160 saying they had had a great year growing wheat. Brother Green, we're going to pay you all your back salary." She gave me a check that night for $160. I gave the check that night at church to Mr. Hendrickson, president of the little bank in Paragon, so he could deposit it for me. I had my personal checks. I decided that on Monday morning I would go and pay the registrar so that I could stay in school.

That night I arrived back in Bloomington. I brought back from my church a suitcase, which was full of apple pie, ham, fried chicken, buns, and cake. My three roommates, A. J. Bachman, Maurice Snider, and Robert "Red" Roth, had the coffee ready. As usual, they drilled me on all my physiology, neuroanatomy, and gross anatomy and helped me get ready for the Monday morning medical quiz. I shared with them the ham and fried chicken, and we had a wonderful session.

Then they asked me the sixty-four dollar question, "Rev., what about the collection? How did you come out?" I assured them that God had heard my prayer, that the Lord had touched a heart over a thousand miles away, away up in Canada, where a big Canadian boy whom I had married to a young lady at Paragon had joined with his wife to send a check to my Paragon church. My roommates could not believe it. They said, "It's incredible. We've never heard of it." I said, "I have the money. I am paid in full."

I could never have finished medical school without the help of my roommates. Eventually, I had the privilege of performing each of their wedding ceremonies.

When I walked into the cadaver lab Monday morning, Joe Davis met me with a whole group, including Dr. Ross, my professor, and said, "We've already heard that your church has given you your back salary. We want to know the story." So that morning I shared with them that the Lord had heard my cry and my prayer and that I had the money.

Medical school gave me many opportunities to witness for the Lord. I married a Catholic boy. I also married Julius Wohlfield, of Jewish origin. Later, he became a Christian. He and his wife, Mary, joined the First Baptist Church of Bedford.

Another boy in my class, Kenneth Hill, also a member of my church at Paragon, fell in love with a little Jewish nurse from the Strauss family, one of the richest families in Indianapolis; they owned the big Strauss clothing store. They asked me to perform their ceremony, and the rabbi was there. They rented the big ballroom of one of the large hotels in Indianapolis. I borrowed a long-tailed tux from Dr. Robert Moore at the Methodist Hospital where I interned, and Jennie borrowed a formal gown from our landlord's daughter-in-law, Ann Arnold. Kenneth's wife became a Christian at the time of the wedding. The family gave me a hundred dollars; back in those days, that was like having a thousand dollars. I said, "Jennie, all I get a whole month for preaching is a hundred. And here in one short thirty-minute service, the family gave me a hundred dollars."

During that freshman year, we formed a worship team. I had about twenty-eight boys in the choir. I remember one Jewish boy in my choir named Jerome Korn. Joe Davis was the song leader. His mother had been a choir leader in Marion, Indiana. We had another boy, Everett Gaunt, who was an organist for the First Baptist Church of Anderson. He played the organ. Jules Heriter read the Scripture, and Everett Gaulke, who later became a missionary to Africa, led in prayer. I had five boys who took the offering: John Westfall, Jim Katterjohn, "Red" Roth, Maurice Snider, and A. J. Bachman.

As first-year medical students, we put on an Easter Sunday night service in 1939 at the First Baptist Church in Bloomington. We put up ads in the student union of Indiana University. Otis Bowen, who later became governor of Indiana, said, "Rev., a lot of the students here on the campus think that medical students are a bunch of crocks or a bunch of drunks. Students will come out of curiosity." We even invited Dean Meyers. He said, "If I don't have any commitments, I will try to come."

I went to the First Baptist Church and talked to the janitor. He said, "Well, Brother Green, on Sunday night we only have a shirttail full. We don't have many come on Sunday night. We had the choir from Franklin Baptist College come one Sunday night, and we only had half of the auditorium full." I said, "We're going to have a church full Sunday night. We're going to advertise all over Bloomington. The pastor is going to announce it Sunday morning." He said, "Oh, I hate to disappoint you, but there won't be many come out Sunday night."

Easter Sunday night came. Joe Davis led the music, Everett Gaunt played the organ, Jules Heriter read the Scripture, and I preached the sermon. The whole auditorium was full of people, including students and members of that church. The janitor had to bring in extra chairs from the Sunday School rooms to seat the crowd. I noticed Dean Meyers was sitting way back. He was not sure what we were going to do or how it was going to turn out. And here were John Westfall, Jim Katterjohn, Arnold Bachman, Maurice Snider, and "Red" Roth. We took a big offering that night, and we gave it all to the church. Joe led the choir in singing "He Arose." The people applauded and said that that was one of the greatest services ever held in that church.

One day at a reunion, Jerome Korn, a Jewish boy, came to me and said, "Rev., don't you ever let my father know that I sat in your choir and sang, 'He Arose. He Arose.'" I assured him I would not tell his dad.

My classmates and I moved to the Indiana University Medical Center in Indianapolis for our last three years. My sophomore year opened, and I was called in by Dr. Rolla Harger and Dr. T. B. Rice, who were counselors for sophomore students. They asked me if I planned to do medical missionary work. I told them that I hoped to go to China. They told me a sad story. They said that preachers' track records at the medical school had not been good. They had already expelled two preacher boys; one had cheated on an exam, and the other had planned to be a medical missionary, but his wife was not sympathetic with his doing that. They had many arguments; they divorced; and finally he had to withdraw. The counselors told me I would have a rough time. After that, I would sit on the front row during every exam so that the monitor could see me and know that what I did was my own work.

I became the roommate of a giant fellow. He had played tackle on the football team of Indiana. He was heavyweight wrestler Bill Sholty. We lived in the home of Bob Ballard, also a student. Everett Gaulky also roomed with us.

I had an old Model A Ford, and we rode to our clinics and to school in the old car. One morning we had a flat. I did not have a jack, so Bill Sholty, the big, 250-pound giant, put his back up to the fender and lifted the car, and we took the wheel off and put on the spare. I do not know how he did it, but we continued on to class that morning .

During my sophomore year, I was nominated and elected president of my class. I beat out John Nill, one of my dear friends. He had been a varsity baseball player, a shortstop. I became president of my medical class, a rarity for a preacher.

That year, Bill Sholty and I drew blood on each other. We did the Wassermann test for syphilis. The whole class did that. In those days we had to incubate the test overnight. We all did as the professor of the lab, Dr. Mazzini, instructed us to do.

The next morning Professor Mazzini went around holding up all the vials, and they were all clear except for one, and that was mine. Mine was cloudy, which meant it was positive for syphilis. Here I was president of my class and the only preacher in my class. Before he came to me and held up the test tube and showed it was cloudy, he first asked me, "I hear you're from Oklahoma. Do you have a gun on you?" I said, "No." He said, "Well, every year we make one come out positive. Last year they ganged up on one of the girls in the class, and she took a towel and beat me over the head with it." He held my test tube up and showed it to the whole class. "What do you think about Rev. Green? He will have to go get treatment for syphilis." He looked at my roommate.

"Bill Sholty, who did this to me?" I asked. "Well, Rev., nobody." I said, "Now, listen, you know mine is negative. You tell me." "Well, during the night several of us slipped into the serology lab here and put some positive serum into your tube, and it came out positive. We felt that would be a good joke." I told him I was glad to be part of their class, and if I needed treatment, I would go to the Long Hospital and start treatment. He said, "Rev., you don't need any treatment. You're okay. You're one of us. We love you."

From then on, as president of their class, as a Baptist preacher, and as their friend, they became my friends. I eventually married sixteen of them.

One was Julius Wohlfield, a Jewish friend in my class. Jennie went with me, and we married them in an apartment. Only his brother showed up because his family did not want him to marry a Gentile girl. His brother was the best man, and Jennie signed the wedding certificate as a witness.

The outstanding wedding ceremony I performed was that for Bob Cannon and his wife, Helen. They were to be married in the Meridian Methodist Church, one of the largest and most beautiful Gothic structures in Indianapolis. By the night of the wedding, we had already rehearsed. Everything was in place. Jim Humphrey, Bob's best friend, was his best man.

When the organ started, we took our places down in front of the altar with the church full of friends and classmates. When the bride came down the aisle on her father's arm, I looked at Bob. I noticed that he was getting pale and that his eyes were blinking. I said, "Jim, I believe Bob's not feeling well." And at that moment Bob collapsed, a big fellow, over two hundred pounds. So Jim Humphrey and I laid him out on the front pew. Helen and her father returned to the back of the sanctuary and stayed there while we revived Bob. We got a wet handkerchief and washed off his face. Bob revived, and Jim and I took him back to the front of the altar. The bride started down the aisle a second time. Bob then fainted a second time. We laid him down, and his father, a big bald-headed fellow from Illinois, said, "You're supposed to be doctors. If you will take him outside where it's cool, he will be better." We took him out the side door and cooled him off. "Are you okay?" I asked. He said, "Yeah, Rev. Let's go."

We returned to the altar, and Helen had already come to the front with her father. I asked, "Who will give the woman in marriage?" Her father said, "Her mother and I." I made the wedding short. I noticed that Bob was beginning to look a little pale, so I said, "Now, let us pray." When the couple knelt on a pillow in front of me, I pushed Bob's head way down so the blood could get to it; then I gave a long prayer. I finished my prayer and said, "Bob, do you feel like getting up?" "Yeah, sure, Rev., sure." They stood up, and I pronounced them husband and wife. They joined their arms and marched out.

Then we all went to a big reception, and all of us medical students surrounded Bob and said, "Bob, do you think we ought to chaperon you on your honeymoon?" He said, "They have given me some warm milk. I'm in good shape." And Bob told me later that he had not eaten all day. He was nervous, and his blood sugar was probably rather low.

On Monday when Bob came back to class, we hoped he would tell us all about his honeymoon; but the professor said, "We will let Bob not tell us his story. You all witnessed his wedding. We think that's enough."

I also married Wally and Jean Bash. They came down to Paragon and wanted to be married in the church there. One other classmate, J. P. Worley, and his wife were with them. Wally and Jean are still married and invited me to their golden wedding anniversary. I also performed a ceremony for Mary Moss, another classmate.

The last Sunday in my church was a long day. I was going to baptize eight men. Emil Ravdin had a brand new car. He came by my apartment in Paragon, picked me up, drove me all the way to Rochester, Indiana, and I married Ollie Hitch, a classmate, and Penny in the church there. We were out at the country club for the big wedding reception on a cold spring day, and Ollie's classmates took him out in his tux and dropped him in the lake. We pulled him out of the water, brought him back into the country club, warmed him up, thawed him out, and wished him well on his honeymoon.

Otis Bowen was an outstanding classmate. After graduation, he moved to Bremen, Indiana, became a family doctor, was elected to the state legislature, became speaker of the house, and served as governor of Indiana for two terms. He and I had become friends and had had our picture taken together during our senior year. We have had similar photos taken during annual reunions.

*Charles E. Green, left, and Otis Bowen as senior medical students at the Indiana University School of Medicine in May 1942. Bowen would later serve as Governor of Indiana and as Secretary of Health and Human Services under President Ronald Reagan.*

Mary Alice Craig was another dear friend in my class. A beautiful lady, she was the queen of our class. (Only eight girls were in my class, and all of them have died except for two, Mary Beal and Mary Moss.) Mary Alice Craig Tucker had a daughter, Marilyn, who later married Dan Price Quayle, and she became the second lady of the nation. When Marilyn came to Lawton one day, I had a picture made with her. I also have a picture of the twenty-fifth reunion of our class. Her mother, who is in that photo, died a few months later with breast cancer.

Some of the happiest days of my life were the four years that I spent in the medical class of 1938 through 1942. I feel that that class was the most unusual one ever graduated from Indiana. We had a future governor, a lady who became the mother of the wife of Dan Quayle, and a Baptist preacher.

After the sophomore year, I moved to a mental health center where I did blood counts and helped take care of patients for

*Charles E. Green, left, and Otis Bowen, Governor of Indiana, attend their thirty-fifth reunion in 1977 as 1942 graduates of the Indiana University School of Medicine. Bowen's note on the photograph reads: "To my classmate, colleague and good friend 'Rev.' Green, fine physician, humanitarian and man of God—with admiration and respect."*

my room and board. That enabled me to continue to tithe and send my mother something every week. During my junior year in medicine at this mental institution, I did a little of everything. I helped take care of the mental patients, including the drunks. In those days they gave an injection of Metrozol when a patient had a seizure. The first time I helped in that, I thought the patient was going to die. He turned blue, but I helped hold his chin up, and the patient did all right and survived.

All during my medical training, I had been corresponding with Jennie Sullivan. Each time I went home, we would go to a show or a picnic and get better acquainted. The senior year was

*Charles E. Green and Marilyn Quayle, in 1992, hold a copy of the twenty-fifth class reunion photo of the May 1942 graduation class of the Indiana University School of Medicine in which both Green and Quayle's mother, Mary Alice Craig (later Tucker) are pictured.*

the time when most of the medical students got married. So late in my junior year, I called her one night and told her I would like to marry her, although the wedding would have to be late in the summer so I could work and save enough money to buy her a wedding ring. She told me she would marry me, and we set the wedding on September 2, 1941, in the First Baptist Church of Lawton.

That summer I was working as interim pastor of the First Baptist Church of Lafayette, Indiana, and the First Baptist Church of Plainfield was available. Kenneth Anderson, the outgoing pastor, told the committee I would like to become pastor there and be near the Methodist Hospital, where I was the intern. I tried out, and the church at Plainfield called me as

*Charles E. Green, third from right on front row, joins with his classmates in attending the fiftieth reunion of their May 1942 graduation from the Indiana University School of Medicine.*

pastor. On the last Sunday in August, I preached the morning service and told them I was heading west to get married, and they gave me a little extra money that morning. I had an old 1931 Model A Ford, but Vincent Appleton, a dear friend who later became pastor at Paragon, let me borrow his new Chevrolet coupe. I headed west, went as far as St. Louis, spent the night, and drove into Lawton on Labor Day.

Then on Tuesday morning, September 2, Jennie and I went to the courthouse and got our marriage license. That night Brother Reid and Brother Wilcoxson married me and Jennie Sullivan. Her dad gave her away, and someone sang "Because." Jennie and I started a long journey together. We traveled as far as Oklahoma City that first night. On the second night, we arrived in Waldron, Scott County, Arkansas, where she had been born. We spent the night with her Uncle Charlie and Aunt Emma Jones. We spent the third night in Memphis. Finally, we arrived back at Plainfield, Indiana, and Mrs. Marie Barlow gave us a room until we could find an apartment of our own.

That was my senior year, and Jennie was able to get a job as secretary. I earned one hundred dollars a month, and she received $125 as secretary. We tithed our incomes. During that year I was accepted as an intern at the Methodist Hospital there in Indianapolis. I continued as pastor of the Baptist church at

*Charles E. Green and Jennie Sullivan on their wedding day, September 2, 1941. They celebrated their fifty-fourth anniversary in 1995.*

Plainfield. Charlotte and Luther Spencer became our dear friends during those two years.

In that year, our first born, Ann-Mary, came along. She was born at Methodist Hospital the same night that Joe Smith's wife was having a baby. I gave the anesthetic for his wife, and he gave the anesthetic for Jennie. Dr. Gustafson delivered Ann-Mary, and we put her in the nursery. I was up all that night giving a transfusion to one of the patients, but made frequent trips to the nursery to look in the incubator at my daughter. The next morning Jennie wanted to know where in the world I had been. I assured her I had been up all night taking care of patients, including our daughter. I told Jennie I would be by to see her more often.

At the end of our internship, all of us were informed that the doctors would have to go out and become a part of the draft. The procurement and assignment board said that every doctor must take a physical. One doctor, Harold Burdette, was turned down for not passing his physical. The board informed me that since I was a preacher, I did not have to be drafted, and that I could stay and do resident work. So I wrote Mayo Clinic. The clinic wrote back and said, "If you can get free from your military entanglements, we want you to become a resident in pediatrics at the Mayo Clinic in Rochester, Minnesota."

On July 1, 1943, as I was nearing the end of my internship, I debated what to do. I wanted to do pediatrics. I could avoid going into the service since I was classified as a preacher, but I tore up the letter and threw it away. Eager to join the United States Army, I went out to Fort Harrison and took my physical.

CHAPTER 7

# Medical Residency and Military Service

A FEW WEEKS LATER, I RECEIVED A LETTER saying I had been commissioned as a first lieutenant in the Medical Corp, and I was to report the first week of June. As one of the first in my class to go into the service, I was instructed to report to Carlisle Barracks in Harrisburg, Pennsylvania, in June 1943 for my basic training. At the hospital, the chief of staff heard that I had received orders, and he let me off a week early and told me to take my family out to Oklahoma. So Jennie and I and our little seven-month-old Ann-Mary rode in an old 1932 Model A Ford and headed for Oklahoma to visit her mother and my mother before I was inducted in the service. Jennie also became pregnant with our second born, Larry. The day came when I preached my last sermon at Plainfield.

I had been trying to win to Christ several of the men there. One of them, George Bryant, and his wife Fern, had been especially friendly to me and Jennie. Past fifty years of age, he, as well as his boy, Ralph, were not Christians. Fern had said,

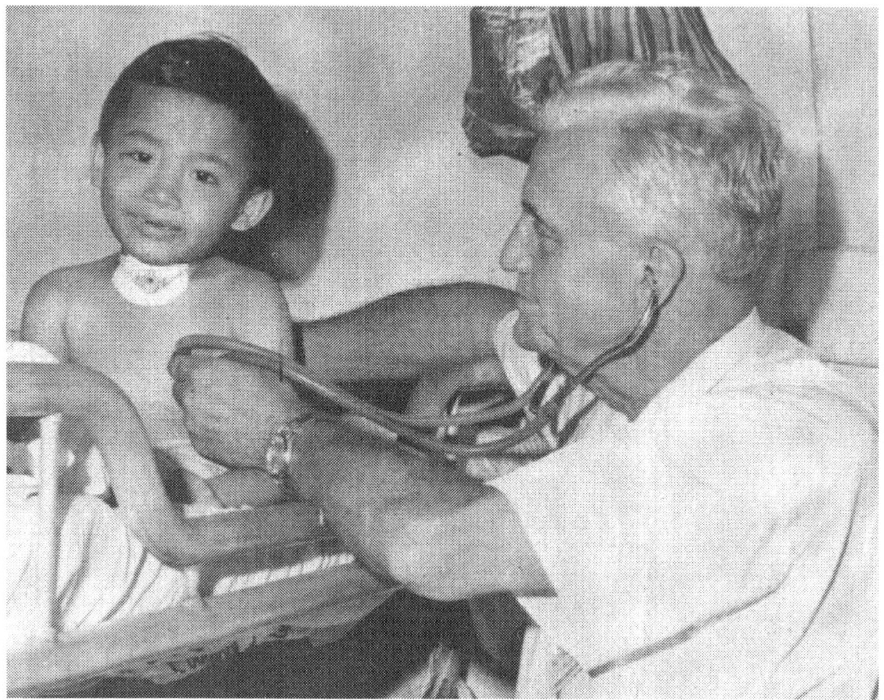

*Charles E. Green, Lawton pediatrician, and participant in the American Medical Association's Volunteer Physician for Vietnam Program, examines a Vietnamese patient in the Children's Hospital in Hue, Vietnam, in the summer of 1969.*

"Help me win them both to Christ." And Ivan Albright, the coach of the high school football team, was not a Christian. That last Sunday morning I preached, all of these men came forward: the football coach, George, and his boy, Ralph. I baptized them that night.

The next day George and his wife, Fern, took me and Jennie to the train station. I caught a train for Carlisle Barracks and started my Army career with boot training.

Before I finished the course, at about four weeks, I was called out with several others and told, "You boys have orders to report to the clearing station, to turn in your equipment." We got on a train and rode to Charleston, South Carolina, and were put in a medical pool at Stark General Hospital. I called Jennie and said, "I want you and Ann-Mary to come down to Charleston and see me."

During World War II, America had the greatest spirit of togetherness I have ever experienced. Later, when I went to Vietnam as a volunteer doctor, in the summer of 1969, it seemed the whole nation was falling apart. We were in a great controversy.

After a week, Jennie, Ann-Mary, and I rode a train all the way back to Indianapolis. The long passenger train was full of soldiers and other people traveling. Every four hours I had to go through seventeen cars to get to the dining car to warm Ann-Mary's bottle. We were on that train all day and all night and got into Indianapolis the next day. We were glad to get home.

In August I had to return to New Orleans to the port of embarkation. On the night our troop ship was to leave, they told us not to go out to eat but to get our duffel bags ready. They loaded up forty-three of us doctors and took us to the port to the big troop ship. We were assigned to the library, where they had put triple-deck beds. That troop ship had over two thousand soldiers on it, but we did not know where we were going. The ship moved out in the South Atlantic, and we were informed that we were going to the West Indies, some of us to Trinidad and others to Puerto Rico. The war was on.

*Charles E. Green as a second lieutenant in the United States Army while stationed in Puerto Rico in the mid-1940s.*

Our only fear was of the U-boats in that area. One night about midnight, the captain of the ship told us to put on our life jackets and to be ready in case a torpedo hit us. They turned off all the motors, and we sat there as a dead ship for over an hour. Finally, our captain said that an escort had come from Guantánamo Bay to protect us. That night was a long night, for the captain said, "Now, if we get hit, don't jump overboard because this old crate will float." When morning came, we resumed our trip. It took us eleven days to go from New Orleans to San Juan, Puerto Rico. We zigzagged to avoid being hit by one of the German submarines.

One day they asked several of us doctors to go down to the bottom of the ship. As we descended, I noticed that water was dripping from the walls. I asked somebody, "What does this mean?" They said, "Well, we're below the water line." I said, "I would be scared to death to sleep down here. If a torpedo hit, we would all be gone." That night, I said, "Thank you, Lord, I hope we don't get hit."

After several days on the South Atlantic, the troop ship landed in San Juan, Puerto Rico. We were assigned to the Rodriquez General Hospital, where I served as a medical officer on the second floor of the medical ward.

During that first year in Puerto Rico, I left Jennie in Indianapolis carrying a boy, I hoped. Sure enough, I received a cablegram one morning that my boy had at last arrived. He had been born on October 23, 1943, at the Methodist Hospital in Indianapolis. We named him Lawrence Charles, "Larry" for short. He would later become a medical doctor.

After six months in the Rodriquez Hospital, I was sent to Camaguey, Cuba, to replace a doctor at a little air base, which served both the Navy and the Army. Pilots from this base patrolled the South Atlantic because the United States had lost over four hundred ships in that area. While I was there, the commanding officer put in for a promotion for me. One day I received a letter that I had been promoted to captain, and that was a great day because it gave me a boost in money. I felt that God Almighty had had a hand in helping me because I was the first in my group of forty-three doctors to be shipped to Puerto Rico to receive a promotion.

I met some important people on our base. One day Batista, the President of Cuba, came to our base and visited with us. He had lost his leadership and had to go into exile. Also at that little base, I had the brief privilege of being a doctor to Bob Hope. One night we were informed that Hope and his whole group were going to visit our base as a last stop. They had been to North Africa. They arrived by plane in June 1944, and we took them to a hangar where they presented the USO program that night. The USO troop said they were hungry, so we took them to our small PX and gave them hamburgers and milk shakes.

That night, I sat down with Bob Hope. He was working out his passport and visa and came to the line which said, "Sex." He looked at me and said, "Captain Green, what's sex? I've been away from Dolores for several months." I said, "When you get home, I'm sure Dolores will give you a basic lesson." And then I helped him fill it out.

Hope said, "I have here a lot of beautiful things that I bought when we stopped in the Virgin Islands, especially lace and linens. I hope they let me in. We're going into Miami. They always check everything I bring back."

Hope also told me that he had a sty on his right eye. While we were waiting for a plane, I put hot packs on his eye. He said "I've been doing that ever since I left North Africa." I said, "Well, it doesn't feel like a sty. It feels like a cyst." He said, "That's strange. About a year ago, I had a cyst removed from the other eye." I told him that cysts are bilateral. Usually, if you have one in one eye, you will have one in the other eye. He said, "Thanks, Dr. Green for looking me in the eye." I did not realize that I had taken care of one of the outstanding men in the show business, a celebrity. That night the USO troop boarded the plane and went back to the United States, landing in Miami, Florida.

A few months later I was shipped back to San Juan, Puerto Rico, replaced by a Navy doctor who was to take over our air base. After a few more months, V-day came and I was able to have my family join me. Jennie and both children arrived. A fellow and his wife, who had run out of gasoline stamps, had taken them all the way to Miami in exchange for the stamps, and my family had caught an Army plane and landed in San Juan. I met them, took them to Henry Barracks, and we had a wonderful time getting reacquainted. Then they let me and Jennie take a trip to the Virgin Islands for a week of rest and recreation. There she became pregnant with Jane Ellen. Soon

*Charles and Jennie Green and their children, Ann-Mary and Lawrence Charles (Larry), send a Christmas greeting from Puerto Rico in 1945 while he was stationed there in the United States Army.*

after that, one day they announced that I had enough points to come back and be discharged. It only took us four days to come home on the ship, although it had taken eleven days to go down because we had to avoid the submarines.

Jennie vomited most of the way home because she was both seasick and a few months pregnant. We landed in New Orleans and rode the Rock Island back to Lawton, Oklahoma. Her mother met us, and we lived with her until we bought a little house at 407 Bell.

Then after practicing in Lawton for a few months, I told Jennie that I wanted to do a residency in pediatrics. I left by train in May 1946 for Washington, D.C., to start my residency in Children's Hospital, leaving Jennie, who was pregnant with Janie, and the other two children in Lawton. I stayed in the intern and resident quarters for a few months trying to find a house. Everything was filled up. I could not find a vacancy anywhere in Washington, D.C. At Children's Hospital everyone tried to help me. Then one day someone asked me to preach at the Brookland Baptist Church. I preached there, and they called me as interim pastor. I did not ask them how much salary I was to get; instead, I asked if I could move my family. They said yes.

I gladly accepted. I made forty dollars a month as a resident and ninety dollars a month as pastor, and the church gave us a place to live.

I went back to Oklahoma and picked up my little family after Jane Ellen was born, and we traveled to Washington, D.C., and lived in a parsonage until spring. After the Brookland Church called a pastor, we had to vacate the parsonage. Some members of the church told me that they had a little summer home, a log cabin over one hundred years old, in Silver Spring, Maryland. They let us have that little log cabin. Looking back, I wonder at the courage we had. Without heat we lived there from April to October, and the weather was continually cold and damp. Our only source of heat was an electric stove on which Jennie boiled water. And none of us had a cold. God is good!

The area was wonderful with many big trees, lilac bushes, and a green forest with wild raspberries. I had enough money to buy a small wading pool for my children. I bought a slide and added a swing that went out over the valley. Some of our happiest days were spent there in that log cabin.

Then an invitation came to go to Richmond to be associated with Dr. Ambrose McGee, another pediatrician. Also, I had an opportunity to go to the Southern Baptist Foreign Mission Board in Richmond to inquire as to when the door would open for me to go to China as a medical missionary. A dear friend, Welch Wampler, loaned me fifteen hundred dollars to pay down on a house in Richmond, and we moved there to begin practice. Soon I realized that I wanted to finish my residency in pediatrics, which I lacked by about four months. I received an opportunity at the Medical College of Virginia to finish these months, which would qualify me for the American Board of Pediatrics and enable me to take the American Board exam. This would also enable me to go to the Foreign Mission Board and check on the possibility of my becoming a medical missionary.

In May 1948 I was finishing my residency. We sold our house, and I took Jennie and the children to Indiana to stay with some dear friends, Luther and Charlotte Spencer. That same month, Baker James Cauthen of the Foreign Mission

Board came to the Children's Hospital where I was finishing my residency. He had just come back from Shanghai. He said, "You will never get to China. The communists are overrunning it. I'm on my way to Memphis to speak at the Southern Baptist Convention. I'm going back to China to pick up my family because we're having to evacuate all the mission areas in China." All of them were evacuated except Bill Wallace, who was tortured and killed by the communists while in prison.

CHAPTER 8

# Medical Career

JULY 1948 CAME. I FINISHED MY AMERICAN BOARD exam in pediatrics, went back to Plainfield and picked up my family, and we journeyed to Lawton. Earlier we had bought a little house at 407 Bell, and that was where I started my medical practice.

Upon returning to Lawton, I learned that Miss Lily Stafford, my chemistry teacher at Lawton High School, 1928–1930, was still driving a 1929 Chevrolet sedan. With the help of Dr. Byron Aycock and Dr. Bill Cole, we started a campaign among her former students to raise enough money to purchase Miss Stafford a new car. Dean Phillips, the Chevrolet agent, gave us a hundred dollars on the 1929 model and also gave us a large discount price on a new car. We raised sixteen hundred dollars and on Thanksgiving Day, 1949, we presented the car to her as a surprise at the football game between Clinton High School and Lawton High School.

As the first pediatrician in Lawton, I was busy from day one. A new hospital was soon built. In 1951 I became the first chief of staff of Comanche County Memorial Hospital and also chief of pediatrics. A wonderful future in medicine lay ahead.

71

*Charles E. Green launches his medical practice in Lawton, Oklahoma, in the fall of 1948.*

In the summer of 1954, the polio patients in Southwest Oklahoma came to Comanche County Memorial Hospital, and at one time I had over forty children with acute polio. That was a long summer, and I was up many nights. Also, my son, Larry, who is now a doctor, came down with Bulbur Polio, and I had to hold him while my partner, Dr. Roy Donaghe, did the spinal tap, which was positive. But Larry fully recovered.

I lost two patients that summer. One was Danny Mains, a big six-foot, four-inch boy, who played center on the basketball team from Altus, Oklahoma. I prayed with him and talked to his dad, but when his temperature went to 107, I had to inform

*New Chevrolet presented to Lily Stafford, retired chemistry teacher at Lawton High School, on Thanksgiving Day, 1949, by left to right: Bill Cole, Byron Aycock, Dean Phillips, and Charles E. Green.*

the family that I was losing the battle. Danny died at about 3:00 the next morning.

In 1957 many of us attended the American Academy of Pediatrics in Miami, Florida, and Jonas Salk demonstrated his polio vaccine. The field trials in Pittsburgh, Pennsylvania, his home city, had been successful, and he told us he felt the vaccine was safe, and that we could use it. I took in as my partner Dr. Melton Meek, and we spent many days giving that vaccine to children brought to our office.

In 1962 the oral vaccine for polio was developed. That year I led a polio vaccination campaign for Southwest Oklahoma, and we gave the oral polio vaccine on a cube of sugar to every student in Lawton and Comanche County, Cotton County, Tillman County, and Jackson County. I feared that somebody might come down with polio as a result of the oral vaccine, but fortunately none did.

Years earlier, we were living at 407 Bell. In the fall of 1949, I was out in the front yard in the late afternoon playing with Larry and Ann-Mary. Coach Glenn Dosser came by the house about 6:00. He stopped his car, leaned out the window, and said, "Dr. Green, would you like to sit on the bench with the Lawton High Wolverines tonight? We need a doctor to sit on the bench with us." I accepted his invitation. That night I had the privilege of sitting on the sidelines of Roosevelt Stadium with the football team of 1949 for the opening game. I have been there ever since. For forty-seven years I have been team physician for the Lawton High Wolverines.

I want to thank Glenn Dosser for that invitation to witness. Every year I try to tell these young men about how Christ can make a difference in their lives. What an opportunity I have had to be a witness: a witness in seminary, in medical school, and in Lawton, Oklahoma.

One day Coach Bo Bowman called me and said, "Dr. Green, we want you and your wife to come to Lawton High. We are having a reception for you." At the end of the reception, he told us that he had cleared it with the school board and the state legislature to name the practice field at Lawton High in my honor.

*Three generations of Lawton High School Wolverines: Charles E. Green, center; son Larry Green, a physician; and grandson George Horton. (Photograph by Brammer Studio, Lawton, Oklahoma. Used by permission.)*

Thank you, Coach Bowman. I have lived through nine coaches, and they have all been great. They have allowed me to lead the team in prayer at the opening of the game and at the close. I have had pure joy as the team physician for all of these years for Lawton High, Eisenhower High, and McArthur High.

Also, I would like to thank Coach Darrell Aschlager and his staff. They sent my name to the Oklahoma High School Coaches Association, and I was voted into the Hall of Fame in 1986 in Tulsa, Oklahoma. That night was a great night for me and my family. We attended the banquet. I was inducted into the Oklahoma Coaches Association Hall of Fame as the only physician ever to have that distinguished honor.

CHAPTER 9

# The Gracious, Wonderful Hoosiers

I WOULD LIKE TO THANK ALL OUR FRIENDS IN Indiana, especially the churches that stood with me for eight years helping me earn my Master of Theology degree at the Southern Baptist Theological Seminary in 1937 and my M.D. at Indiana University School of Medicine in 1942, followed by a year of rotating internship at the Methodist Hospital in Indianapolis.

One of the greatest friends I ever had was George A. Ritchey, a Mississippi boy. He helped me secure a scholarship to the seminary. When he was called to the First Baptist Church of Lafayette, Indiana, he took me to Paragon, Indiana, and both introduced me to the churches and recommended me to become their pastor. All the churches had a call session, and I was invited to return to Paragon on July 1, 1935, as pastor at Paragon, New Salem, and Samaria Baptist Churches.

On July 4, 1935, I preached my first service at New Salem Baptist Church, a rural church, four miles south of Paragon. I only preached the first Sunday of each month. This little country church grew in numbers, and soon we had over a hundred people present the first Sunday of each month.

Some of the people who paid my salary of fifteen dollars on each first Sunday of the month included Jim and Zula Burnett, a wonderful couple who raised one daughter and five boys. Jim was the treasurer of the church, and sometimes he gave me eighteen dollars instead of fifteen, for he said he had put his son Arthur through medical school and knew the costs.

I lived in the home of Charles and Eva Baker. Many happy meals were shared in that home. They had two children. Other families who shared their home and meals were Clint and Flossie Hodges, Curt and Effie Wampler, the Thomas family and the Beaman family. One of the first men whom I won to Christ was Charley Whitesell. His wife, Ida, invited me to their home in August 1935. He had a terminal illness, and I visited his home and shared the gospel with him. After several months, he accepted Christ; later, I preached his funeral at New Salem Baptist Church.

On Sunday, July 11, 1935, I preached my first sermon at Paragon Baptist Church, a half-time church, which meant we had a preaching service two Sundays a month. Paragon was a village of three to four hundred people, and we averaged seventy to ninety people in Sunday School and worship services. We spent Sunday afternoons on Imogene and James Farr's farm playing baseball. They were two dear people who stood by me and helped me pastor the Paragon Baptist Church.

Other helpful persons included Aunt Alice Whitaker, who gave me a room in which to live, keep my books, and study the year I went to Indiana University Medical School. My next-door neighbor was Granddad Earl Applegate; he always had a smile, and his two children, Blan and Beryle, were dear friends. Blan and Janice Cherry awakened me early one Monday morning and asked me to marry them that day. I united them in marriage, and they took me back to the seminary at Louisville. They have been married over fifty years, and it is a real joy to visit with them when we have a reunion in Paragon. Also, I want to thank Mr. R. E. Hendrickson, who taught the men's Sunday School class. As president of the Paragon State Bank, he loaned me the money that I sent to Indiana University Medical School

*Charles E. Green enjoys a laugh with Pauline Hendrickson, member of the Paragon Baptist Church in Paragon, Indiana.*

to hold my place as a student the first year. His wife, son Julius, and two daughters Lorene and Pauline helped keep the church doors open. So did Phyllis Jean Alexander and her mother June. Carolyn Holsapple Wiley and her mother Helen were also faithful workers in the church.

In the last fifty years, my contact with Paragon Baptist Church has been through the efforts of Pauline Hendrickson. Helena Randall, the treasurer of the church, played a wonderful and helping role in my receiving a check to help me pay my tuition the second semester at Indiana University.

On Sunday, July 18, 1935, I preached my first sermon at Samaria Baptist Church as pastor. Samaria is about twelve miles northwest of Paragon, and it was a quarter-time church, which meant that I preached only one Sunday each month. Alice and Charlie Dow and their two children Harry and Bessie took care of me at Samaria. They gave me a room in their home, fed me many meals, and helped take care of my laundry. Through the years, I have enjoyed my visits in Paragon with that family. Archie and Blanche Burnett have kept Samaria Church going, along with the Stierwalts, the Noah Bland family, the Wilson family, and Jan Whitaker.

With the help of Aaron and Bliss Myers, we started a Saturday night mission at Whitaker Baptist Church. In Whitaker I spent many happy hours and enjoyed many good meals in the home of Mildred Alexander and her mother and dad. I also have

*Charles E. Green, center, reunites with friends in Gosport, Indiana, left to right: Mary Ann Sensney, Julie Bonness, Barbara Bonness, Mary Wampler, Bobby Bonness, and Sue Alice Stouder.*

fond memories of the Hite Family, Mildred and Duane, and Evelyn Vickrey, who sang many specials at Whitaker Church. Families at Gosport, Indiana, deserving mention include Attie Asher, a friend of Aunt Alice Whitaker, who had two daughters, Edith and Mary Asher. Edith married Herman Bonness, and this family, including their daughter and son, Mary Ann and Bobby, have always supported me. Bobby and his dad met my plane in Indianapolis and escorted me to Whitaker to preach the funeral for Aaron Myers. Mary and Welch Wampler and their daughters, Jane and Sue Alice, helped me financially through the years, and we could not ask for better friends.

In July 1941, I was called as pastor of Plainfield Baptist Church in Indiana. After a brief honeymoon, Jennie and I started our first home. Marie Barlow let us stay in her home until we could rent an apartment.

Charlotte and Luther Spencer helped take care of Jennie, Ann-Mary, and Larry while I was in the service. Their children were Ray, Betty Jo, and David. I appreciate their ministry to us.

CHAPTER 10

# The Last Prescription

VIOLENCE IS A MONUMENTAL PROBLEM THAT affects every aspect of today's society. On April 19, 1995, a great tragedy took place in the bombing of the Federal Building in Oklahoma City, Oklahoma. Dozens of people, including children, lost their lives. The greatest outpouring of human compassion and sympathy that I have ever witnessed quickly resulted. Doctors, nurses, firemen, police, and other workers, including Governor Keating of Oklahoma, went to the area to see if they could help. President Clinton and his wife went to Oklahoma, as did Dr. Billy Graham, to help start the healing.

This tragedy has been a wake-up call. We need to unite together to help each other and to pray for one another. The catalyst that has brought us together is that fact that innocent children in a day-care center in the bombed building were killed by ruthless, insensitive, evil workers. I have raised five children and now have sixteen grandchildren and one great-grandchild, Braelyn Ann Johnson, and they are all precious.

America is awake now. We need to join together and fight for the freedom, the safety, and the security of our families.

*Federal Building in Oklahoma City, Oklahoma, bombed on April 19, 1995.*

Because of the magnitude of the problem of violence in our country, our homes, and our schools, which might lead us to despair and a feeling of paralysis, we must mobilize together. There must be a breakthrough in overcoming teenage pregnancy, escalating juvenile crime, and the falling apart of our homes because of the increase in divorces. Thirty percent of our children are living in single-parent homes, and eighty percent of the people in prison are school dropouts.

So where do we start and how do we approach the problem? There are no quick solutions or easy fixes. Even the outstanding pediatrician of our day, Dr. Benjamin Spock, states that he does not know all the answers. I would like to offer my humble and simple prescription for today's overwhelming problems.

My prescription results from fifty years of practicing as a pediatrician, walking the sidelines of high school football games for forty-seven years, serving as a team physician for three senior-high teams, serving as a medical consultant to the Lawton Public Schools, serving as attending physician for the

Comanche County Detention Center, and having been blessed with five children of my own, including two registered nurses and one medical doctor. My son is a family practitioner in Carnegie, Oklahoma. One daughter is a social worker, and another daughter is a school teacher. And do not forget my sixteen grandchildren.

Here is my final prescription, which, I feel with the cooperation of our homes, schools, churches, civic organizations, doctors, lawyers, and law officials, can provide a breakthrough if we return to the basics and learn the value and necessity of old-fashioned hard work.

When my mother awakened us one morning in September 1925, she informed us that our father had gone to California for work, and we had not heard from him for several months. We had to face the stark reality that our only hope and final option to survive was to "hit the cotton patch." We all pitched in and went to work picking cotton for our survival. In my mother's days there was no welfare system, no Department of Human Services, and no food stamps to help a needy family.

I belong to a large Kiwanis Civic Club in Lawton, and our international motto is, "The first priority is the child." Also, the Optimist Club has a motto, "As a friend of the boy." Recently, I received a letter form the American Medical Association stating that the AMA has decided to project a campaign against family violence. This campaign can help communities if the home, the church, the school, doctors, lawyers, civic organizations, and law-abiding officials will join hearts and hands in finding a solution to one of the major problems of the twentieth century.

During high school football games, many teams join hands when they are on the offense, when they come back to the huddle and wait for the quarterback to give the signal of the play. I like that concept. It shows that all eleven boys are joining together to block together, to try to open a hole for the fullback to run through for a touchdown and win the game. If we can mobilize all the positive influences in every community uniting together in one voice to stop violence, united together in one voice for the health of our  children, united in one voice for healthy teenagers, united in one voice for effective parenting, then we can make enormous progress for good.

We need to realize today that the resources of God are still available. And with his help, the gift of the Holy Spirit, we can all join hearts and hands and work together and pray together and have a community free of drug abuse and free of violence in the home and the school. So my final prescription is this: I would ask all of us to ask God for help—every individual, every family, every school, every organization, and every church.

# Appendixes

# Appendix A

## MY FAVORITE SCRIPTURES

*John 3:16**

> For God so loved the world, that he gave his only begotten Son, that whosoever believeth in him should not perish but have everlasting life.

**This was the first verse that I memorized in Sunday School at age twelve. My teacher was Mrs. Asa Wilson.*

*Philippians 4:13*

> I can do all things through Christ which strengtheneth me.

*Philippians 4:19*

> My God shall supply all your need according to his riches in glory by Christ Jesus.

*Philippians 1:21*

> For me to live is Christ and to die is gain.

# Appendix B

## A Tribute to My Classmates

Many times I have been asked by my Hoosier friends how a genuine "Oakie," especially a Southern Baptist preacher, was accepted into the freshman class of Indiana University (IU) Medical School in September 1938. My answer is simple—the Lord opened the doors and by the grace and help of Almighty God, I graduated four years later with an M.D. Let me share with you some of the men and women in this class who gave me sincere encouragement and generous help to complete the tough four-year course.

Will Kurtz will always be my number-one "hero" in that class. We were classmates for four years, and then we were interns at the Methodist Hospital. During my year of internship, I also was pastor of the Plainfield Baptist Church. Every other Sunday, I was on duty at the hospital and had to cover all emergencies on one particular floor. I would leave the hospital and drive to the Baptist church for the A.M. and P.M. services. In order to preach at those two services, I would have to get someone to cover my floor for any medical emergencies. Will Kurtz came to my rescue and took the calls while I was conducting the church worship hours. Will did this for me an entire year. One Sunday night when I returned to the hospital, Will said, "Rev., you had six new admissions to your floor, and I have admitted them and completed their medical histories."

What a friend Will Kurtz was. He died prematurely as the result of a house call to a sick Vietnam veteran. He was trying to draw a blood sample from the patient, who became enraged. During the ensuing scuffle, Will stuck himself with the needle and died a few days later from a deadly virus. I would say he died in the line of duty. If this book becomes a financial success, I intend to set up a scholarship fund at IU Medical School in his memory. Will ministered to me in ways I will never forget.

Our class was unusual in that one of our classmates, Otis Bowen, became a two-term governor of Indiana and also Secretary of Health and Human Services under President Ronald Reagan. Otis Bowen and I had a picture made when we were seniors in 1942 in front of Emerson Hall at Indiana University. We also had our picture taken together at subsequent class reunions. One can tell by recent pictures that we are senior citizens. (See chapter six for several photos.)

The queen of our class was Mary Alice Craig, who was beautiful and a good student. Several times she would say to me, "Rev., hang in there, and one of these days we will graduate." Little did I dream that someday her daughter, Marilyn Quayle, would be the second lady of the land. When Marilyn visited Lawton, Oklahoma, and was campaigning for George Bush and her husband, Dan Quayle, I was fortunate to have a visit with her and shared with her the picture, which included her mother, of the twenty-fifth class reunion of our 1942 IU Medical School graduating class. (See photo in chapter six.) That was the last time I saw Mary Alice Craig Tucker, for she died a few months later with breast cancer.

There were two characters in my class, Welbon D. Britton and Wally Bash, who were always full of jokes and good humor. At the noon hour, we often had lunch together. They kept us laughing and probably saved us from mental depression. "Britt" was the clown of our class. Libby and Jean will have two stars in heaven for living with these two characters.

During my freshman year in medical school, I roomed with A. J. Bachman, Maurice Snider, and Robert "Red" Roth. Each Sunday night when I returned from my church at Paragon, they drilled me in gross anatomy, necroanatomy, and physiology and helped prepare me for Monday morning class exams. In return, I shared with them the cake, pie, and ham that I brought from my church.

Bill Sholty was my roommate the second year of medical school. I married Bill and Mary Sholty; they have remained our dear friends since we graduated in that wonderful 1942 class.

In order for a man who was an ordained minister to become a practicing physician, he had to have the support of his family. My

*Twenty-fifth reunion of 1942 Indiana University Medical School graduating class, with three graduates standing, left to right: Bill and Mary Sholty, George and Lois Godersky, and Charles and Jennie Green.*

family of five children have always given wholehearted support.

Jennie, my wife, is the strength behind any success I have accomplished. Her commitment to the Bible, me, and our children is a daily encouragement to me. Jennie and I agreed early in our marriage that we would tithe our income and give the Lord the first fruits of our labor. When I was selling newspapers and she was working at a Kress Store, our total tithe was about thirty cents per week. During our first years of marriage, our tithe was about twenty dollars per month. Now, we give much more than the stipulated ten percent tithe to our church each week. Plus we are faithful in giving to other religious and worthwhile causes. Giving is our greatest joy. The Lord has opened the windows of heaven, and he has richly blessed our home.

# Appendix C



## CLASSMATES WHOSE WEDDINGS I HAVE CONDUCTED

A. J. Bachman
Wallace Bash
Joe Buchmeier
Merle Bundy
Robert Cannon
Colin Elliott
Ed Hawk
Kenneth Hill
Ollie Hitch
Robert Jordan
Don McCartney
Mary Moss
Robert Peacock
Robert "Red" Roth
William Sholty
Joe Shugart
Maurice Snider
Julius Wohlfield

# Appendix D

*Charles E. Green, chairman of the Board of Trustees of Oklahoma Baptist University, installs Grady C. Cothen as president in September 1966. Cothen would later serve as president of New Orleans Baptist Theological Seminary and then as president of the Southern Baptist Sunday School Board.*